Chinese Cantonese Cooking

Chinese Cantonese Cooking

DEH–TA HSIUNG

||| •PARRAGON• |||

First published in Great Britain in 1994 by
Parragon Book Service Ltd
Unit 13-17, Avonbridge Trading Estate
Atlantic Road
Avonmouth
Bristol BS11 9QD

ISBN 1 85813 634 2

Printed in Italy

Acknowledgements:

Design & DTP: Pedro & Frances Prá-Lopez / Kingfisher Design
Art Direction: Pedro Prá-Lopez
Managing Editor: Alexa Stace
Photography: Amanda Heywood
Cover Photography: Clive Streeter
Cover Step-by-Step Photography: Karl Adamson
Home Economist: Deh-Ta Hsiung
Stylist: Marian Price

Gas Hob supplied by New World Domestic Appliances Ltd
Photographs on pages 6, 18, 26, 56 & 66: Tony Stone Images

Note:
Cup measurements in this book are for American cups. Tablespoons are assumed to be 15ml.

Contents

CHAPTER ONE

Appetizers

A number of dishes in Cantonese cooking are served as an appetizer – just like hors d'oeuvres in the West. One of the advantages of these dishes is that they are generally prepared and cooked well in advance – hours or even days before serving. Also, almost all the dishes selected here are ideal for a buffet-style meal or as party food. Instead of serving different appetizers individually, try serving a small portion of each together as an assorted hors d'oeuvres. Select a minimum of three or four different items: Crispy Spring Rolls, Butterfly Prawns (Shrimp), Barbecue Spare Ribs, Barbecue Pork (Char Siu), and so on.

Other dishes from the Main Course section that can be served as a part of the appetizer are Sweet and Sour Prawns (Shrimp), Lemon Chicken, and Baked Crab with Ginger and Spring Onions (Scallions). Remember not to have more than one of the same type of food – the ingredients should be chosen for their harmony and balance in colour, aroma, flavour and texture.

Opposite: A Chinese cook at an open-air stall in Xinjiang province. Wayside stalls selling takeaway food are a common sight all over China, offering wontons, spare ribs, prawns, spring rolls and other tasty snacks for hungry workers.

STEP 3

STEP 4

STEP 5

STEP 6

CRISPY VEGETARIAN SPRING ROLLS

For a non-vegetarian version, just replace mushrooms with chicken or pork, and the carrots with prawns (shrimps).

MAKES 12 ROLLS

125 g/4 oz fresh bean-sprouts, washed and drained
60 g/2 oz spring onions (scallions)
60 g/2 oz carrots
60 g/2 oz canned sliced bamboo shoots, rinsed and drained
60 g/2 oz mushrooms
2-3 tbls vegetable oil, plus oil for deep-frying
$^{1}/_{2}$ tsp salt
$^{1}/_{2}$ tsp sugar
1 tbsp light soy sauce
1 tsp Chinese rice wine or dry sherry
12 spring roll skins, defrosted if frozen
1 tbsp cornflour (cornstarch) paste (see page 77)
flour, for dusting
vegetable oil, for deep-frying

1 Cut all the vegetables into thin shreds roughly the same size and shape as the bean-sprouts.

2 Heat the oil in a hot wok and stir-fry the vegetables for about 1 minute. Add the salt, sugar, soy sauce and wine and continue stirring for 1½-2 minutes. Remove the vegetables from the wok with a slotted spoon and place in a bowl. Drain off the excess liquid then leave to cool.

3 To make the spring rolls, place about 2 tablespoons of the vegetables one-third of the way down on a skin, with the triangle pointing away from you.

4 Lift the lower flap over the filling and fold in one end.

5 Roll once and fold in the other end.

6 Roll once more, brush the upper edge with a little flour paste, and roll into a neat package. Lightly dust a tray with flour and place the spring roll with the flap-side down. Make the rest of the spring rolls in the same way.

7 Heat the oil in a wok or deep-fryer until smoking, then reduce the heat to low and deep-fry the spring rolls in batches for 2-3 minutes or until golden and crispy. Remove with a slotted spoon and drain on paper towels. Serve hot with a dip sauce such as soy sauce, sweet and sour sauce or chilli sauce.

BUTTERFLY PRAWNS (SHRIMP)

Use unpeeled, raw king or tiger prawns (shrimp) which are about 7-10cm (3-4in) long.

STEP 1a

SERVES 4

12 raw tiger prawns (shrimp) in their shells
2 tbsp light soy sauce
1 tbsp Chinese rice wine or dry sherry
1 tbsp cornflour (cornstarch)
2 eggs, lightly beaten
8-10 tbsp breadcrumbs
vegetable oil, for deep-frying
salt and pepper
shredded lettuce leaves, to serve
chopped spring onions (scallions), to garnish

1 Shell and devein the prawns (shrimp) but leave the tails on. Split them in half from the underbelly about halfway along, leaving the tails still firmly attached.

2 Mix together the salt, pepper, soy sauce, wine and cornflour (cornstarch) in a bowl, add the prawns (shrimp) and turn to coat. Leave to marinate for 10-15 minutes.

3 Heat the oil in a preheated wok. Pick up each prawn (shrimp) by the tail, dip it in the beaten egg then roll it in the breadcrumbs to coat well.

4 Deep-fry the prawns (shrimp) in batches until golden brown.

Remove them with a slotted spoon and drain on paper towels.

5 To serve, arrange the prawns (shrimp) neatly on a bed of lettuce leaves and garnish with spring onions (scallions), either raw or soaked for about 30 seconds in hot oil.

STEP 1b

VARIATIONS

Butterfly prawns (shrimp) may also be served on a bed of crispy seaweed. This classic Chinese accompaniment provides the perfect foil for the luscious prawns (shrimp). Dried seaweed can be bought in packets from Oriental stores and supermarkets. Follow the instructions on the packet to prepare it.

STEP 3a

TO DEVEIN LARGE PRAWNS (SHRIMP)

First remove the shell. Make a shallow cut about three-quarters of the way along the back of each prawn (shrimp), then pull out and discard the black intestinal vein.

STEP 3b

11

STEP 1

STEP 2

STEP 3

STEP 4

LETTUCE-WRAPPED MINCED MEAT

The original version of this recipe uses quail or pigeon meat.
Serve the minced meat and lettuce leaves on separate dishes:
each guest then wraps his or her own parcel.

SERVES 4

250 g/8 oz minced pork or chicken
1 tbsp finely chopped Chinese mushrooms
1 tbsp finely chopped water chestnuts
pinch of sugar
1 tsp light soy sauce
1 tsp Chinese rice wine or dry sherry
1 tsp cornflour (cornstarch)
2-3 tbsp vegetable oil
1/2 tsp finely chopped ginger root
1 tsp finely chopped spring onions
  (scallions)
1 tbsp finely chopped Szechuan preserved
  vegetables (optional)
1 tbsp oyster sauce
a few drops of sesame oil
salt and pepper
8 crisp lettuce leaves, to serve

1 Mix the minced meat with the mushrooms, water chestnuts, salt, pepper, sugar, soy sauce, wine and cornflour (cornstarch).

2 Heat the oil in a preheated wok or pan and add the ginger and spring onions (scallions) followed by the meat. Stir-fry for 1 minute.

3 Add the Szechuan preserved vegetables and continue stirring for

1 more minute. Add the oyster sauce and sesame oil, blend well and cook for 1 more minute. Remove to a warmed serving dish.

4 To serve: place about 2-3 tablespoons of the mixture on a lettuce leaf and roll it up tightly to form a small parcel. Eat with your fingers.

SZECHUAN PRESERVED VEGETABLES

These pickled mustard roots are hot and salty, with a peppery flavour, and are often used to intensify the spiciness of a dish. Once opened, store in the refrigerator in a tightly sealed jar.

STEP 1

STEP 2

STEP 3

STEP 4

BARBECUE SPARE RIBS

This is a simplified version of the half saddle of pork ribs seen hanging in the windows of Cantonese restaurants. Use the specially small, thin ribs known as finger ribs.

SERVES 4
OVEN: 230°C/450°F/GAS 8;
THEN 200°C/400°F/GAS 6

500 g/1 lb pork finger spare ribs
1 tbsp sugar
1 tbsp light soy sauce
1 tbsp dark soy sauce
3 tbsp hoi-sin sauce
1 tbsp rice wine or dry sherry
4-5 tbsp water or Chinese Stock (see page 76)
mild chilli sauce, to dip
coriander leaves, to garnish

1 Trim off any excess fat from the ribs and cut into pieces. Mix the ribs with the sugar, light and dark soy sauce, hoi-sin sauce and wine in a baking dish, and marinate for about 2-3 hours.

2 Add the water or stock to the ribs and spread them out in the dish. Roast in a preheated hot oven for 15 minutes.

3 Turn the ribs over, lower the heat and cook for 30-35 minutes longer.

4 To serve, chop each rib into 3-4 small, bite-sized pieces with a large knife or Chinese cleaver and arrange on a serving dish. Pour the sauce from the baking dish over them, garnish with coriander leaves, and serve with chilli sauce as a dip.

HOI-SIN SAUCE

This sweet, thick sauce is made from soybean flour, soy beans, vinegar, sesame seed oil, chilli, sugar, salt, garlic and spices. It is sold in cans and jars; if you buy it in a can, store it in a glass bottle in the refrigerator once opened, where it will keep for several months. It is ideal for use in marinades and as a dip or condiment for many Chinese dishes.

SPARE RIBS

Ask your local butcher to cut some if you can't find the right size of ribs in the supermarket. Don't throw away any trimmings from the ribs – they can be used for soup or stock.

STEP 1

STEP 2

STEP 4

STEP 5

BARBECUE PORK (CHAR SIU)

Also called honey-roasted pork, these are the strips of reddish meat
sometimes seen hanging in the windows of Cantonese restaurants.

SERVES 4
OVEN: 220°C/425°F/GAS 7;
THEN 180°C/350°F/GAS 4

500 g/1 lb pork fillet
150 ml/¼ pint/⅔ cup boiling water
1 tbsp honey, dissolved with a little hot
  water

MARINADE:
1 tbsp sugar
1 tbsp crushed yellow bean sauce
1 tbsp light soy sauce
1 tbsp hoi-sin sauce
1 tbsp oyster sauce
½ tsp chilli sauce
1 tbsp brandy or rum
1 tsp sesame oil
shredded lettuce, to serve

1 Cut the pork into strips about 2.5
cm/1 in thick and 18-20 cm/7-8 in
long and place in a large shallow dish.
Add the marinade ingredients and turn
the pork until well coated. Cover, and
leave to marinate for at least 3-4 hours,
turning occasionally.

2 Remove the pork strips from the
dish with a slotted spoon, reserving
the marinade. Arrange the pork strips on
a rack over a baking tin (pan). Place the

tin (pan) in the preheated oven and pour
in the boiling water. Roast for about 10-
15 minutes.

3 Lower the oven temperature. Baste
the pork strips with the reserved
marinade and turn. Roast for a further
10 minutes.

4 Remove the pork from the oven,
brush with the honey syrup, and
lightly brown under a medium hot grill
(broiler) for 3-4 minutes, turning once or
twice.

5 To serve, allow the pork to cool
slightly before cutting it. Cut across
the grain into thin slices and arrange on
a bed of shredded lettuce. Make a sauce
by boiling the marinade and the
drippings in the baking tin (pan) for a few
minutes, strain and pour over the pork.

CHAPTER TWO

Soups

Soup is not normally served as a separate course in China, except at formal occasions and banquets – and then it usually appears towards the end of the meal.

At an everyday meal in Chinese homes, a simply made soup, almost always a clear broth in which a small amount of thinly sliced or shredded vegetables and/or meat have been poached quickly, is served with the other dishes in the meal.

If a good stock is not available, as is often the case in Chinese homes, a Chinese housewife would just stir-fry the ingredients first in a little oil, then add water and seasonings (salt, soy sauce or monosodium glutamate) to make an instant soup fit for the gods!

If you use a chicken stock cube, remember to reduce the amount of seasonings in the recipes, since most commercially-made stock cubes are fairly salty and spicy. It is always worth making your own Chinese Stock (see page 76) if you have the time.

Opposite: *Father and son enjoy a bowl of soup with wontons in a Shanghai restaurant. In China soup is usually served with other dishes as part of a meal, not a separate starter as in the West.*

SWEETCORN & CRAB MEAT SOUP

You must use American-style creamed sweetcorn for this soup since it originated in the USA! Chicken can be used instead of the crab meat, if preferred.

STEP 1

SERVES 4

125 g/4 oz crab meat
¼ tsp finely chopped ginger root
2 egg whites
2 tbsp milk
1 tbsp cornflour (cornstarch) paste (see
   page 77)
600 ml/1 pint/2 ½ cups Chinese Stock (see
   page 76)
1 x 250 g/8 oz can American-style creamed
   sweetcorn
salt and pepper
finely chopped spring onions (scallions), to
   garnish

1 Flake the crab meat (or coarsely chop the chicken breast) and mix with the ginger.

2 Beat the egg whites until frothy, add the milk and cornflour (cornstarch) paste and beat again until smooth. Blend in the crab or chicken.

3 In a wok or large frying pan (skillet), bring the stock to the boil, add the creamed sweetcorn and bring back to the boil.

4 Stir in the crab meat or chicken pieces and egg-white mixture,

adjust the seasoning and stir gently until the mixture is well blended. Serve hot, garnished with chopped spring onions (scallions).

STEP 2

CHOOSING CRAB

Always obtain the freshest possible crab; fresh is best, though frozen or canned will work for this recipe. The delicate, sweet flavour of crab diminishes quickly: this is why many Chinese cooks make a point of buying live crab.

STEP 3

CREAMED SWEETCORN

Although sweetcorn is not unknown in Asia today, it really is a Western food by tradition. Be sure to use proper creamed sweetcorn for this soup, as it has quite a different texture from the more usual sweetcorn kernels. Creamed sweetcorn has a thick, slightly mushy consistency, makng a thick, creamy soup.

STEP 4

STEP 1

STEP 2

STEP 3

STEP 5

SEAFOOD & TOFU SOUP

*Use prawn (shrimp), squid or scallops, or a combination
of all three.*

SERVES 4

*250 g / 8 oz seafood: peeled prawns
    (shrimp), squid, scallops, etc. defrosted if
    frozen
¹/₂ egg white, lightly beaten
1 tbsp cornflour (cornstarch) paste (see
    page 77)
1 cake tofu (bean curd)
750 ml / 1 ¹/₄ pints / 3 cups Chinese Stock (see
    page 76)
1 tbsp light soy sauce
salt and pepper
fresh coriander leaves, to garnish (optional)*

1 Small prawns (shrimp) can be left
whole; larger ones should be cut
into smaller pieces; cut the squid and
scallops into small pieces.

2 If raw, mix the prawns (shrimp)
and scallops with the egg white
and cornflour (cornstarch) paste to
prevent them from becoming tough
when they are cooked.

3 Cut the cake of tofu into about 24
small cubes.

4 Bring the stock to a rolling boil.
Add the tofu and soy sauce, bring
back to the boil and simmer for 1 minute.

5 Stir in the seafood, raw pieces first,
pre-cooked ones last. Bring back to
boil and simmer for just 1 minute. Adjust
the seasoning and serve garnished with
coriander leaves, if liked.

FRESH CORIANDER
(CILANTRO)

The musky, sharp scent and flavour of
fresh coriander (cilantro) is truly
distinctive. When buying it fresh, look for
bright green, unwilted leaves. To store it,
wash and dry the leaves and leave them
on the stem. Wrap the leaves in damp
kitchen paper and keep them in a plastic
bag in the refrigerator.

TOFU

Tofu, also known as bean curd, is an
almost tasteless substance made from
puréed yellow soya beans, which are
very high in protein. It is widely available
in supermarkets, and Oriental and health-
food stores. It is sold in cakes about
7.5 cm / 3 in square.

STEP 1

STEP 2

STEP 3

STEP 4

MIXED VEGETABLE SOUP

Select 3 or 4 of the suggested vegetables for this soup: the Chinese like to blend different colours, flavours and textures in order to create harmony as well as contrast.

SERVES 4

*about 30-60 g/1-2 oz each of mushrooms,
   carrots, asparagus, mangetout (snow
   peas), bamboo shoots, baby sweetcorn,
   cucumber, tomatoes, spinach, lettuce,
   Chinese leaves, bean curd etc.
600 ml/1 pint/2 ½ cups Chinese Stock (see
   page 76)
1 tbsp light soy sauce
a few drops of sesame oil (optional)
salt and pepper
finely chopped spring onions (scallions), to
   garnish*

1 Cut your selection of vegetables into roughly uniform shapes and sizes (slices, shreds or cubes).

2 Bring the stock to a rolling boil in a wok and add the vegetables, bearing in mind that some require a longer cooking time than others: add carrots and baby sweetcorn first, cook for 2 minutes, then add asparagus, mushrooms, Chinese leaves, bean curd, and cook for another minute.

3 Spinach, lettuce, watercress, cucumber and tomato are added last. Stir, and bring the soup back to the boil.

4 Add soy sauce and the sesame oil, and adjust the seasoning. Serve hot, garnished with spring onions (scallions).

SESAME OIL

Sesame oil is a low-saturate oil widely used for its nutty, aromatic flavour. This rich-flavoured oil is made from the toasted sesame seeds and used as a seasoning, not as a cooking oil. Thick and dark, it burns easily, so it should be added at the last moment, just before serving. It makes a wonderful dressing for salads when diluted with other vegetable oils. A few drops are often added to soups and other dishes just before serving – it can often be seen on the surface, as in the photograph opposite.

CHAPTER THREE

Main Course Dishes

The main course dishes in a conventional Chinese meal are usually stir-fried or braised. Certain dishes may require a longer cooking time and, strictly speaking, belong to a separate course – known as the principal dish – and should be served independently.

Stir-frying meat and fish dishes have become very popular in Western kitchens in recent years. This is because these dishes are comparatively simple and easy to prepare and cook, as well as being economical, delicious and healthy. Basically, the ingredients are cut into small, thin slices or shreds, then tossed and stirred in hot oil over high heat for a very short time. Thus the natural flavours, as well as the subtle textures, of the food are preserved. When correctly done, the meats (which include fish and poultry) should be tender and juicy, and the vegetables crisp and bright – over-cooking will render the food into a tasteless soggy mess.

Opposite: *Work is finished for the day, and a cook in XinJiang sells noodles for the evening meal. It takes years to learn the art of making noodles and the products of specialist noodle-makers are greatly sought after.*

SWEET & SOUR PRAWNS (SHRIMP)

Use raw prawns (shrimp) if possible; ready-cooked ones can be added to the sauce without the initial deep-frying (step 2).

STEP 1

STEP 2

STEP 3

STEP 4

SERVES 4

300-350 g/10-12 oz raw king or tiger prawns (shrimp) in their shells
vegetable oil, for deep-frying
fresh coriander leaves, to garnish

SAUCE:
1 tbsp vegetable oil
2 tsp finely chopped spring onions (scallions)
1 tsp finely chopped ginger root
1 tbsp light soy sauce
2 tbsp sugar
3 tbsp rice vinegar
1 tsp Chinese rice wine or dry sherry
125 ml/4 fl oz/¹/₂ cup Chinese Stock (see page 76) or water
1 tbsp cornflour (cornstarch) paste (see page 77)
a few drops of sesame oil
coriander leaves, to garnish

1 Remove the legs from the prawns (shrimp) but leave the body shell.

2 Heat the oil in a preheated wok. Deep-fry the prawns (shrimp) in hot oil for about 45-50 seconds, or until they become bright orange. Remove with a slotted spoon and drain on paper towels.

3 To make the sauce, heat the oil in a preheated wok and add the spring onions (scallions) and ginger, followed by the seasonings, sugar and stock or water. Bring to the boil.

4 Add the prawns (shrimp) to the sauce, blend well, then thicken the sauce with the cornflour (cornstarch) paste. Stir until smooth and add the sesame oil.

5 Serve hot, garnished with coriander leaves.

SWEET AND SOUR SAUCE

It is now possible to buy readymade sweet and sour sauce in bottles. They are really handy if you are short of time, but they are no match for the homemade version, which has a much subtler flavour.

FRIED SQUID FLOWERS

*The addition of green (bell) pepper and black bean sauce to the squid
makes a colourful and delicious dish from the Cantonese school.*

STEP 2

STEP 3

STEP 4

STEP 5

SERVES 4

350-400 g/12-14 oz prepared and cleaned
   squid (see below)
1 medium green (bell) pepper, cored and
   seeded
3-4 tbsp vegetable oil
1 garlic clove, finely chopped
¼ tsp finely chopped ginger root
2 tsp finely chopped spring onions
   (scallions)
½ tsp salt
1 tsp Chinese rice wine or dry sherry
2 tbsp crushed black bean sauce
a few drops of sesame oil

1 If ready-prepared squid is not
available, prepare as instructed
below right.

2 Open up the squid and score the
inside of the flesh in a criss-cross
pattern.

3 Cut the squid into pieces about the
size of an oblong postage stamp.
Blanch in a bowl of boiling water for a
few seconds. Remove and drain; dry well
on paper towels.

4 Cut the (bell) pepper into small
triangular pieces. Heat the oil in a

preheated wok and stir-fry the (bell)
pepper for about 1 minute. Add the
garlic, ginger, spring onion (scallion),
salt and squid. Continue stirring for
another minute.

5 Finally add the black bean sauce
and wine, and blend well. Serve
hot, sprinkled with sesame oil.

TO CLEAN THE SQUID

Clean the squid by first cutting off the
head. Cut off the tentacles and reserve.
Remove the small soft bone at the base of
the tentacles and the transparant
backbone, as well as the ink bag. Peel off
the thin skin, then wash and dry well.

STIR-FRIED PRAWNS (SHRIMP)

This colourful and delicious dish is cooked with vegetables:
vary them according to seasonal availability.

STEP 1

SERVES 4

60 g/2 oz mangetout (snow peas)
½ small carrot, thinly sliced
60 g/2 oz baby sweetcorn
60 g/2 oz straw mushrooms
175-250 g/6-8 oz raw tiger prawns
*   (shrimp), peeled*
1 tsp salt
½ egg white, lightly beaten
1 tsp cornflour (cornstarch) paste (see
*   page 77)*
about 300ml/½ pint/1 ¼ cups vegetable oil
1 spring onion (scallion), cut into short
*   sections*
4 slices ginger root, peeled and finely
*   chopped*
½ tsp sugar
1 tbsp light soy sauce
1 tsp Chinese rice wine or dry sherry
a few drops of sesame oil

1 Top and tail the mangetout (snow peas); cut the carrot into the same size as the mangetout (snow peas); halve the baby sweetcorn and straw mushrooms.

2 Mix the prawns (shrimp) with a pinch of the salt, the egg white and cornflour (cornstarch) paste.

3 Heat a wok over high heat for 2-3 minutes, then add the oil and heat to medium hot before adding the prawns (shrimp); stir to separate them. Remove with a slotted spoon as soon as the colour changes.

4 Pour off the oil, leaving about 1 tablespoon in the wok. Add all the vegetables and stir-fry for about 1 minute. Add the prawns (shrimp) and the seasonings. Blend well. Sprinkle with the sesame oil and serve hot.

STEP 2

STEP 3

VEGETABLE SELECTION

When choosing alternative vegetables, remember to select contrasting colours and textures, as shown here – one green, one orange, one yellow etc.

STEP 4

33

STEP 1

STEP 2

STEP 3

STEP 4

BAKED CRAB WITH GINGER

The crab is interchangeable with lobster. In Chinese restaurants, only live crabs and lobsters are used, but ready-cooked ones can be used at home quite successfully.

SERVES 4

1 large or 2 medium crabs, weighing about
    750 g/ 1½ lb in total
2 tbsp Chinese rice wine or dry sherry
1 egg, lightly beaten
1 tbsp cornflour (cornstarch)
3-4 tbsp vegetable oil
1 tbsp finely chopped ginger root
3-4 spring onions (scallions), cut into sections
2 tbsp light soy sauce
1 tsp sugar
about 75 ml/ 5 tbsp/⅓ cup Chinese Stock (see
    page 76) or water
½ tsp sesame oil
coriander leaves, to garnish

1 Cut the crab in half from the under-belly. Break off the claws and crack them with the back of the cleaver or a large kitchen knife.

2 Discard the legs and crack the shell, breaking it into several pieces. Discard the feathery gills and the stomach sac. Place in a bowl with the wine, egg and cornflour (cornstarch) and leave to marinate for 10-15 minutes.

3 Heat the oil in a preheated wok and stir-fry the crab with ginger and spring onions (scallions) for 2-3 minutes.

4 Add the soy sauce, sugar and stock or water, blend well and bring to the boil. Cover and cook for 3-4 minutes, then remove the cover, sprinkle with sesame oil and serve.

TECHNIQUES

The term "baked" may be used on Chinese restaurant menus to describe dishes such as this one, which are actually cooked in a wok. "Pot-roasted" may be a more accurate way to describe this cooking technique.

BUYING CRABS

Crabs are almost always sold ready-cooked. The crab should feel heavy for its size, and when it is shaken, there should be no sound of water inside. A good medium-sized crab should yield about 500 g/1 lb meat, enough for 3-4 people.

FISH WITH BLACK BEAN SAUCE

Any firm and delicate fish steaks such as salmon or turbot can be cooked by the same method.

SERVES 4-6

1 sea bass, trout or turbot, weighing about 675g/1½ lb, cleaned
1 tsp salt
1 tbsp sesame oil
2-3 spring onions (scallions), cut in half lengthways
1 tbsp light soy sauce
1 tbsp Chinese rice wine or dry sherry
1 tbsp finely shredded ginger root
1 tbsp oil
2 tbsp crushed black bean sauce
2 finely shredded spring onions (scallions)
fresh coriander leaves, to garnish (optional)
lemon slices, to garnish

1 Score both sides of the fish with diagonal cuts at 2.5cm (1in) intervals. Rub both the inside and outside of the fish with salt and sesame oil.

2 Place the fish on top of the spring onions (scallions) on a heat-proof platter. Blend the soy sauce and wine with the ginger shreds and pour evenly all over the fish.

3 Place the fish on the platter in a very hot steamer (or inside a wok on a rack), cover and steam vigorously for 12-15 minutes.

4 Heat the oil until hot, then blend in the black bean sauce. Remove the fish from the steamer and place on a serving dish. Pour the hot black bean sauce over the whole length of the fish and place the shredded spring onions (scallions) on top. Serve garnished with coriander leaves and lemon slices.

STEP 2

STEP 3

FISH STEAKS

If using fish steaks, rub them with the salt and sesame oil, but do not score with a knife. The fish may require less cooking, depending on the thickness of the steaks – test for doneness with a skewer after about 8 minutes.

STEP 4

STEP 1

STEP 2

STEP 3

STEP 4

CHICKEN FOO-YUNG

Strictly speaking, a foo-yung dish (the name means white lotus petals) should use egg whites only to create a very delicate texture. But most people associate foo-yung with an omelette in Chinese restaurants.

SERVES 4

175 g/6 oz chicken breast fillet, skinned
½ tsp salt
pepper
1 tsp rice wine or dry sherry
1 tbsp cornflour (cornstarch)
3 eggs, beaten
½ tsp finely chopped spring onions (scallions)
3 tbsp vegetable oil
125 g/4 oz green peas
1 tsp light soy sauce
salt
few drops of sesame oil

1 Cut the chicken across the grain into very small, paper-thin slices, using the cleaver. Place the slices in a shallow dish, add the ½ teaspoon salt, pepper, wine and cornflour (cornstarch) and turn in the mixture until they are well coated.

2 Beat the eggs in a small bowl with a pinch of salt and the spring onions (scallions).

3 Heat oil in a preheated wok, add chicken slices and stir-fry for about 1 minute, making sure that the slices are kept separated. Pour the beaten eggs over the chicken, and lightly scramble

until set. Do not stir too vigorously, or the mixture will break up in the oil. Stir the oil from the bottom of the wok so that the foo-yung rises to the surface.

4 Add the peas, salt and soy sauce and blend well. Sprinkle with sesame oil and serve.

VARIATION

If available, chicken *goujons* can be used for this dish: these are small, delicate strips of chicken which require no further cutting and are very tender.

LEMON CHICKEN

Lemon sauce is a Cantonese speciality, easily available from Oriental stores, or you can make your own.

STEP 1

SERVES 4

350 g/12 oz chicken breast fillets, skinned
1 tbsp rice wine or dry sherry
1 egg, beaten
4 tbsp plain flour blended with 2 tbsp water
vegetable oil, for deep-frying
readymade lemon sauce, or homemade sauce
  (see right)
salt and pepper
slices of fresh lemon, to garnish

1 Cut the chicken into thin slices and place in a shallow dish with wine, salt and pepper. Leave to marinate for 25-30 minutes.

2 Make a batter with the egg and flour paste. Place the chicken slices in the batter and turn to coat well.

3 Heat the oil in a wok or deep-fryer. Deep-fry the chicken slices until golden brown, remove with a slotted spoon and drain on paper towels. Cut the chicken slices into bite-sized pieces.

4 Heat about 1 tablespoon of oil in a wok or pan. Stir in the lemon sauce until well blended and pour evenly over the chicken. Garnish with lemon slices and serve.

LEMON SAUCE:

1 tbsp vegetable oil
250 ml/8 fl oz/1 cup Chinese Stock (see
  page 76)
1 tbsp caster sugar
1 tbsp lemon juice
1 tbsp cornflour (cornstarch)
1 tsp salt
1 tsp lemon rind

Heat the oil in a wok until hot, reduce the heat and add all the other ingredients. Blend well, then bring to the boil and stir until smooth.

STEP 2

STEP 3

READYMADE SAUCES

Many readymade sauces are now available, and they are very useful if you are short of time. However, try to find time to make this homemade lemon sauce which has a delicious fresh taste.

STEP 4

41

STEP 1

STEP 2

STEP 3

STEP 4

CHICKEN WITH BEAN-SPROUTS

This is the basic Chicken Chop Suey to be found in almost every Chinese restaurant and takeaway all over the world.

SERVES 4

125 g/4 oz chicken breast fillet, skinned
1 tsp salt
¹/₄ egg white, lightly beaten
2 tsp cornflour (cornstarch) paste (see page 77)
about 300 ml/¹/₂ pint/ 1 ¹/₄ cups vegetable oil
1 small onion, thinly shredded
1 small green (bell) pepper, cored, seeded and thinly shredded
1 small carrot, thinly shredded
125 g/4 oz fresh bean-sprouts
¹/₂ tsp sugar
1 tbsp light soy sauce
1 tsp rice wine or dry shrerry
2-3 tbsp Chinese Stock (see page 76)
a few drops of sesame oil
chilli sauce, to serve

1 Thinly shred the chicken and mix with a pinch of the salt, the egg white and cornflour (cornstarch) paste.

2 Heat the oil in a preheated wok and stir-fry the chicken for about 1 minute, stirring to separate the shreds. Remove with a slotted spoon and drain on paper towels.

3 Pour off the oil, leaving about 2 tablespoons in the wok. Add all the vegetables except the bean-sprouts and stir-fry for about 2 minutes, then add the bean-sprouts and stir for a few seconds.

4 Add the chicken with the remaining salt, sugar, soy sauce and wine, blend well and add the stock or water. Sprinkle with the sesame oil and serve at once.

CHICKEN CHOP SUEY

Chop Suey actually originated in San Francisco at the turn of the century when Chinese immigrants were first settling there, and was first devised as a handy dish for using up leftovers.

STEP 1

STEP 2

STEP 3

STEP 4

CHICKEN WITH MUSHROOMS

Dried Chinese mushrooms (Shiitake) should be used for this dish –
otherwise use black rather than white fresh mushrooms.

SERVES 4

300-350 g/10-12 oz chicken, boned and
*   skinned*
¹/₂ tsp sugar
1 tbsp light soy sauce
1 tsp rice wine or dry sherry
2 tsp cornflour (cornstarch)
4-6 dried Chinese mushrooms, soaked in
*   warm water*
1 tbsp finely shredded ginger root
salt and pepper
a few drops of sesame oil
coriander leaves, to garnish

1 Cut the chicken into small bite-
sized pieces and place in a bowl.
Add the sugar, soy sauce, wine and
cornflour (cornstarch) and leave to
marinate for 25-30 minutes.

2 Drain the mushrooms and dry on
paper towels. Slice the mushrooms
into thin shreds, discarding any hard
pieces of stem.

3 Place the chicken pieces on a heat-
proof dish that will fit inside a
bamboo steamer. Arrange the
mushroom and ginger shreds on top of
the chicken and sprinkle with salt,
pepper and sesame oil.

4 Place the dish on the rack inside a
hot steamer or on a rack in a wok
filled with hot water and steam over high
heat for 20 minutes. Serve hot, garnished
with coriander leaves.

CHINESE MUSHROOMS

Chinese mushrooms come in many
varieties: Shiitake are the best, and the two
terms are often used synonymously. These
fragrant mushrooms are most readily
available at Oriental food stores and
supermarkets but are also seasonally
available.
Do not throw away the soaking water from
the dried Chinese mushrooms. It is very
useful, as it can be added to soups and
stocks to give extra flavour.

DUCK WITH PINEAPPLE

For best results, use ready-cooked duck meat, widely available from Chinese restaurants and takeaways.

STEP 1

STEP 2

STEP 3

STEP 4

SERVES 4

125-175 g/4-6 oz cooked duck meat
3 tbsp vegetable oil
1 small onion, thinly shredded
2-3 slices ginger root, thinly shredded
1 spring onion (scallion), thinly shredded
1 small carrot, thinly shredded
125 g/4 oz canned pineapple, cut into small slices
¹/₂ tsp salt
1 tbsp red rice vinegar
2 tbsp syrup from the pineapple
1 tbsp cornflour (cornstarch) paste (see page 77)
black bean sauce, to serve (optional)

1 Cut the cooked duck meat into thin strips.

2 Heat the oil in a preheated wok, add the shredded onion and stir-fry until the shreds are opaque. Add the ginger, spring onion (scallion) and carrot shreds. Stir-fry for about 1 minute.

3 Add the duck shreds and pineapple to the wok together with the salt, rice vinegar and the pineapple syrup. Stir until the mixture is blended well.

4 Add the cornflour (cornstarch) paste and stir for 1-2 minutes until the sauce has thickened. Serve hot.

CANNED PINEAPPLE

Fortunately, most canned fruit is now available preserved in juice rather than syrup. The sugared syrup once used exclusively for this purpose was cloyingly sweet. To prepare this dish, be sure to choose pineapple in juice rather than syrup, so that the sauce is pleasantly tangy rather than overwhelmingly sugary.

RED RICE VINEGAR

Red rice vinegar is made from fermented rice. It has a distinctive dark colour and depth of flavour. If unavailable, use red wine vinegar, which is similar in flavour.

STIR-FRIED PORK WITH VEGETABLES

This is a basic "meat and veg" recipe – the meat can be either pork, chicken, beef or lamb, and the vegetables can be varied according to seasonal availability.

STEP 1

STEP 2

STEP 3

STEP 4

SERVES 4

*250 g/8 oz pork fillet, sliced
1 tsp sugar
1 tbsp light soy sauce
1 tsp rice wine or dry sherry
1 tsp cornflour (cornstarch) paste (see page 77)
1 small carrot
1 small green (bell) pepper, cored and seeded
about 175 g/6 oz Chinese leaves
4 tbsp vegetable oil
1 spring onion (scallion), cut into short sections
a few small slices of peeled ginger root
1 tsp salt
2-3 tbls Chinese Stock (see page 77) or water
a few drops of sesame oil*

1 Thinly slice the pork fillet into small pieces and place in a shallow dish. Add half the sugar and the soy sauce, the wine and cornflour (cornstarch) paste, and leave in the refrigerator to marinate for 10-15 minutes.

2 Cut the carrot, green (bell) pepper and Chinese leaves into thin slices roughly the same length and width as the pork pieces.

3 Heat the oil in a preheated wok and stir-fry the pork for about 1 minute to seal in the flavour. Remove with a slotted spoon and keep warm.

4 Add the carrot, (bell) pepper, Chinese leaves, spring onion (scallion) and ginger and stir-fry for about 2 minutes.

5 Add the salt and remaining sugar, followed by the pork and remaining soy sauce, and the stock or water. Blend well and stir for another 1-2 minutes until hot. Sprinkle with the sesame oil and serve.

ALTERNATIVES

This dish can be made with other meats, as mentioned in the introduction. If using chicken strips, reduce the initial cooking time in the wok as the chicken will take less time to cook

STEP 1

STEP 2

STEP 3

STEP 4

SWEET AND SOUR PORK

This has to be the most popular Chinese dish all over the world.
The pork can be replaced with almost any other ingredient:
fish, prawns (shrimp), chicken or even vegetables.

SERVES 4

250-300 g/8-10 oz lean pork
2 tsp brandy or whisky
vegetable oil, for deep-frying
1 egg, beaten
2 tbsp plain flour
salt and pepper

SAUCE:
1 tbsp vegetable oil
1 small onion, cut into small cubes
1 small carrot, cut into small cubes
½ small green (bell) pepper, cored, seeded
  and cut into small cubes
1 tbsp light soy sauce
3 tbsp sugar
3 tbsp wine vinegar
1 tbsp tomato purée (paste)
about 3-4 tbsp Chinese Stock (see page 76)
  or water
1 tbsp cornflour (cornstarch) paste
(see page 77)

1 Cut the pork into small bite-sized cubes. Place in a dish with the salt, pepper and brandy and leave to marinate for 15-20 minutes.

2 Heat the oil in a wok or deep-fryer. Place the pork cubes in a bowl with the beaten egg and turn to coat. Sprinkle on the flour and turn the pork cubes until they are well coated.

3 Deep-fry the pork cubes in batches for about 3-4 minutes, stirring gently to separate the pieces. Remove with a slotted spoon or strainer and drain on paper towels. Reheat the oil until hot, and return the meat to the wok for another minute or so or until golden brown. Remove with a slotted spoon and drain on paper towels.

4 To make the sauce, heat the oil in a pre-heated wok or pan, add the vegetables and stir-fry for about 1 minute. Add the seasonings and tomato purée (paste) with stock or water, bring to the boil and thicken with the cornflour (cornstarch) paste.

5 Add the pork and blend well so that each piece of meat is coated with the sauce. Serve hot.

SPARE RIBS WITH CHILLI

For best results, chop the spare ribs into small bite-size pieces.

STEP 1

SERVES 4

500 g/1 lb pork spare ribs
1 tsp sugar
1 tbsp light soy sauce
1 tsp rice wine or dry sherry
1 tsp cornflour (cornstarch)
about 600 ml/1pint/2 ½ cups vegetable oil
1 garlic clove, finely chopped
1 spring onion (scallion), cut into short
    sections
1 small hot chilli pepper (green or red),
    thinly sliced
2 tbsp black bean sauce
about 150 ml/¼ pint/²/₃ cup Chinese Stock
    (see page 76) or water
1 small onion, cut into small cubes
1 medium green (bell) pepper, cored, seeded
    and cut into small cubes

1 Trim excess fat from the ribs, and
chop each one into 3-4 bite sized
pieces. Place the ribs in a shallow dish
with the sugar, soy sauce, wine and
cornflour (cornstarch) and leave to
marinate for 35-45 minutes.

2 Heat the oil in a preheated wok.
Add the spare ribs and deep-fry for
2-3 minutes until light brown. Remove
with a slotted spoon and drain on paper
towels.

3 Pour off the oil, leaving about 1
tablespoon in the wok. Add the
garlic, spring onion (scallion), chilli
pepper and black bean sauce and stir-fry
for 30-40 seconds.

4 Add the spare ribs, blend well, then
add the stock or water. Bring to the
boil, then reduce the heat, cover and
braise for 8-10 minutes, stirring once or
twice.

5 Add the onion and green (bell)
pepper, increase the heat to high,
and stir uncovered for about 2 minutes to
reduce the sauce a little. Serve hot.

STEP 2

STEP 3

HANDLING CHILLIES

Be very careful when handling and cutting
chilli peppers as they exude a juice which
can cause irritation of the skin. Be sure to
wash your hands after handling, and keep
well away from face and eyes. It is the
seeds of the chilli that are the hottest part
– remove seeds if you do not want a very
hot dish.

STEP 5

STEP 1

STEP 2

STEP 3

STEP 4

OYSTER SAUCE BEEF

Like Stir-fried Pork with Vegetables (page 48) the vegetables used in this recipe can be varied as you wish.

SERVES 4

300 g/10 oz beef steak
1 tsp sugar
1 tbsp light soy sauce
1 tsp rice wine or dry sherry
1 tsp cornflour (cornstarch) paste (see page 77)
½ small carrot
60 g/2 oz mangetout (snow peas)
60 g/2 oz canned bamboo shoots
60 g/2 oz canned straw mushrooms
about 300 ml/½ pint/1¼ cups vegetable oil
1 spring onion (scallion), cut into short sections
2-3 small slices ginger root
½ tsp salt
2 tbsp oyster sauce
2-3 tbls Chinese Stock (see page 76) or water

1 Cut the beef into small, thin slices. Place in a shallow dish with the sugar, soy sauce, wine and cornflour (cornstarch) paste and leave to marinate for 25-30 minutes.

2 Slice the carrots, mangetout (snow peas), bamboo shoots and straw mushrooms so that as far as possible the vegetable pieces are of uniform size and thickness.

3 Heat the oil in a preheated wok and add the beef slices. Stir-fry for about 1 minute, then remove with a slotted spoon and keep warm.

4 Pour off the oil, leaving about 1 tablespoon in the wok. Add the sliced vegetables with the spring onion (scallions) and ginger and stir-fry for about 2 minutes. Add the salt, beef, and the oyster sauce with stock or water. Blend well until heated through, and serve with a dip sauce, if liked.

VARIATIONS

You can use whatever vegetables are available for this dish, but it is important to get a good contrast of colour – don't use all red or all green for example.

CHAPTER FOUR

Vegetables

Being basically an agricultural country, China has really perfected vegetable cooking into a fine art – almost all are cooked for a very short time, thus preserving their natural flavour and texture, as well as the vitamins and the brightness of their colours.

The Chinese eat far more vegetables than meat or poultry, and with a few exceptions, almost all meat and poultry dishes include somc kind of vegetable as a supplementary ingredient – the idea being to give the dish a harmonious balance of colour, aroma, flavour and texture.

When selecting vegetables for cooking, the Chinese attach great importance to the freshness of ingredients used. Always buy crisp, firm vegetables, and cook them as soon as possible. Another point to remember is to wash the vegetables just before cutting, in order to avoid losing vitamins in water, and to cook them as soon as they have been cut so that the vitamin content is not lost through evaporation.

Opposite: A stallholder in Mongolia proudly displays his selection of fruit and vegetables. Chinese cooks attach great importance to freshness, and visit the market daily to buy fresh produce for the family meal.

STEP 1

STEP 2

STEP 3

STEP 4

STIR-FRIED MIXED VEGETABLES

The Chinese never mix ingredients indiscriminately – they are carefully selected to achieve a harmonious balance of contrasting colours and textures.

SERVES 4

60g/ 2 oz mangetout (snow peas)
1 small carrot
125 g/ 4 oz Chinese leaves
125 g/ 4 oz fresh bean-sprouts
60 g/ 2 oz black or white mushrooms
60 g/ 2 oz canned bamboo shoots, rinsed
 and drained
3-4 tbsp vegetable oil
1 tsp salt
1 tsp sugar
1 tbsp oyster sauce or light soy sauce
a few drops of sesame oil (optional)
dip sauce, to serve (optional)

1 Prepare the vegetables: top and tail the mangetout (snow peas), and cut the carrot, Chinese leaves, mushrooms and bamboo shoots into roughly the same shape and size as the mangetout (snow peas).

2 Heat the oil in a preheated wok, and add the carrot first. Stir-fry for a few seconds, then add the mangetout (snow peas) and Chinese leaves and stir-fry for about 1 minute.

3 Add the bean-sprouts, mushrooms and bamboo shoots and stir-fry for another minute.

4 Add the salt and sugar, continue stirring for another minute, then add the oyster sauce or soy sauce, blend well, and sprinkle with sesame oil (if using). Serve hot or cold, with a dip sauce, if liked.

OYSTER SAUCE

This sauce, made from oysters cooked together with salt and spices, is used in many Cantonese dishes. It is worth spending a little more on a good bottle of oyster sauce, as the more expensive brands are noticeably better. Good oyster sauce has a rich, almost beefy flavour. Once opened, a bottle of oyster sauce can be kept for months in the refrigerator and used to flavour a range of Oriental dishes.

BEAN-SPROUTS

It is important to use fresh bean-sprouts for this dish – the canned ones don't have the crunchy texture that is vital. If fresh ones are unavailable, select another vegetable, remembering to keep a colour contrast.

STEP 1

STEP 2

STEP 3

STEP 4

BROCCOLI IN OYSTER SAUCE

Some Cantonese restaurants use only the stalks of the broccoli for this dish, for the crunchy texture.

SERVES 4

250-300 g/8-10 oz broccoli
3 tbsp vegetable oil
3-4 small slices ginger root
$\frac{1}{2}$ tsp salt
$\frac{1}{2}$ tsp sugar
3-4 tbsp Chinese Stock (see page 76) or
   water
1 tbsp oyster sauce

1 Cut the broccoli spears into small florets. Trim the stalks, peel off the rough skin, and cut the stalks diagonally into diamond-shaped chunks.

2 Heat the oil in a preheated wok and add the pieces of stalk and the ginger. Stir-fry for half a minute then add the florets and continue to stir-fry for another 2 minutes.

3 Add the salt, sugar and stock or water, and continue stirring for another minute or so.

4 Blend in the oyster sauce. Serve hot or cold.

BROCCOLI STALKS

The broccoli stalks have to be peeled and cut diagonally to ensure that they will cook evenly. If they are thin stalks, the pieces can be added to the wok at the same time as the florets, but otherwise add the stalks first, to ensure that they will be tender.

VARIATION

Any crunchy-textured vegetable can be used in this recipe. If preferred, you could use cauliflower, celery, courgettes, French beans etc, making sure that they are cut into even-sized pieces.

BRAISED CHINESE VEGETABLES

This dish is also known as Lo Han Zhai or Buddha's Delight. The original recipe calls for no less than 18 different vegetables to represent the 18 Buddhas (Lo Han) – but 6-8 are usually quite acceptable.

STEP 1

SERVES 4

5 g/¼ oz dried wood ears
1 cake tofu (bean curd)
60 g/2 oz mangetout (snow peas)
125 g/4 oz Chinese leaves
1 small carrot
90 g/3 oz canned baby sweetcorn, drained
90 g/3 oz canned straw mushrooms, drained
60 g/2 oz canned water chestnuts, drained
300 ml/½ pint/1¼ cups vegetable oil
1 tsp salt
½ tsp sugar
1 tbsp light soy sauce or oyster sauce
2-3 tbsp Chinese Stock (see page 76) or water
a few drops of sesame oil

1 Soak the wood ears in warm water for 15-20 minutes, then rinse and drain, discarding any hard bits, and dry on paper towels.

2 Cut the cake of tofu into about 18 small pieces. Top and tail the mangetout (snow peas). Cut the Chinese leaves and the carrot into slices roughly the same size and shape as the mangetout (snow peas). Cut the baby sweetcorn, the straw mushrooms and the water chestnuts in half.

3 Heat the oil in a preheated wok. Add the tofu and deep-fry for about 2 minutes until it turns slightly golden. Remove with a slotted spoon and drain on paper towels.

4 Pour off the oil, leaving about 2 tablespoons in the wok. Add the carrot, Chinese leaves and mangetout (snow peas) and stir-fry for about 1 minute.

5 Now add the sweetcorn, mushrooms and water chestnuts. Stir gently for 2 more minutes, then add the salt, sugar, soy sauce and stock or water. Bring to the boil and stir-fry for 1 more minute.

6 Sprinkle with sesame oil and serve hot or cold.

STEP 2

STEP 3

WOOD EARS
─────────
Wood ears (a kind of fungus) can usually be obtained in Chinese supermarkets. If unavailable, use another variety of Chinese mushrooms.

STEP 5

STEP 1

STEP 2

STEP 3

STEP 4

STIR-FRIED BEAN-SPROUTS

Be sure to use fresh bean-sprouts, rather than the canned variety, for this crunchy-textured dish.

SERVES 4

250 g/8 oz fresh bean-sprouts
2-3 spring onions (scallions)
1 medium red chilli pepper (optional)
3 tbsp vegetable oil
½ tsp salt
½ tsp sugar
1 tbsp light soy sauce
a few drops of sesame oil (optional)

1 Rinse the bean-sprouts in cold water, discarding any husks or small pieces that float to the top. Drain well on paper towels.

2 Cut the spring onions (scallions) into short sections. Thinly shred the red chilli pepper, if using, discarding the seeds.

3 Heat the oil in a preheated wok. Add the bean-sprouts, spring onions (scallions) and chilli pepper, if using, and stir-fry for about 2 minutes.

4 Add the salt, sugar, soy sauce and sesame oil, if using, to the mixture in the wok. Stir well to blend. Serve hot or cold.

TO GROW BEAN-SPROUTS

It is very easy to grow bean-sprouts. If you find it difficult to buy fresh ones, this could be the answer. Use dried mung beans, obtainable from supermarkets and health-food shops. Wash the beans thoroughly in several changes of water. Place in a lidded jar, or a seed sprouter if you have one, and place in a warm, dark place (the airing cupboard is ideal). Check daily and rinse with a little water to keep them moist. You should have sprouts ready to use in 3-4 days.

VARIATION

The red chilli pepper gives a bite to this dish – leave the seeds in for an even hotter taste. If you prefer a milder, sweeter flavour use red (bell) pepper instead of the chilli pepper. Core, seed and cut into strips in the same way.

CHAPTER FIVE

Rice and Noodles

Rice and noodles provide bulk in the Chinese diet, but the recipes given here are meant to be served on their own, as a light meal or as a snack. For an everyday meal, plain rice is served with two or three other dishes – usually meat and vegetables together with a soup. Fried rice and chow mein are only served at formal occasions, or as a snack between main meals.

In China, noodles are always served at birthday celebrations, as the Chinese consider that the length of noodles symbolizes long life.

The Chinese do not normally conclude an everyday meal with a dessert, but fresh fruit can always be served for those who are used to finishing off a meal with something sweet.

Opposite: *A woman tends the irrigation system in rice paddy fields near Guilin. Rice is the most important staple in the Chinese diet and vast tracts of fertile land are given over to its cultivation.*

STEP 1

STEP 3a

STEP 3b

STEP 5

SEAFOOD CHOW MEIN

*Use whatever seafood is available for this delicious noodle dish –
mussels or crab would also be suitable. Simply add to the
wok with the other seafood in step 6.*

SERVES 4

*90 g/3 oz squid, cleaned
3-4 fresh scallops
90 g/3 oz raw prawns (shrimp), shelled
1/2 egg white, lightly beaten
1 tbsp cornflour (cornstarch) paste (see page
   77)
275 g/9 oz egg noodles
5-6 tbsp vegetable oil
2 tbsp light soy sauce
60 g/2 oz mangetout (snow peas)
1/2 tsp salt
1/2 tsp sugar
1 tsp Chinese rice wine or dry sherry
2 spring onions (scallions), finely shredded
a few drops of sesame oil*

1 Open up the squid and score the
inside in a criss-cross pattern, then
cut into pieces about the size of a postage
stamp.

2 Soak the squid in a bowl of boiling
water until all the pieces curl up.
Rinse in cold water and drain.

3 Cut each scallop into 3-4 slices. Cut
the prawns (shrimp) in half
lengthways if large. Mix the scallops and
prawns with the egg white and cornflour
(cornstarch) paste.

4 Cook the noodles in boiling water
according to the instructions on the
packet, then drain and rinse under cold
water. Drain well, then toss with about 1
tablespoon of oil.

5 Heat 3 tablespoons of oil in a
preheated wok. Add the noodles
and 1 tablespoon of the soy sauce and
stir-fry for 2-3 minutes. Remove to a
large serving dish.

6 Heat the remaining oil in the wok
and add the mangetout (snow
peas) and seafood. Stir-fry for about 2
minutes, then add the salt, sugar, wine,
remaining soy sauce and about half the
spring onions (scallions). Blend well and
add a little stock or water if necessary.

7 Pour the seafood mixture on top of
the noodles and sprinkle with
sesame oil. Garnish with the remaining
spring onions (scallions) and serve hot or
cold.

STEP 1

FRIED NOODLES (CHOW MEIN)

This is a basic recipe for Chow Mein. Additional ingredients such as chicken or pork etc can be added if liked.

SERVES 4

275 g/9 oz egg noodles
3-4 tbsp vegetable oil
1 small onion, finely shredded
125 g/4 oz fresh bean-sprouts
1 spring onion (scallion), finely shredded
2 tbsp light soy sauce
a few drops of sesame oil

1 Cook the noodles in salted boiling water according to the instructions on the packet (usually no more than 4-5 minutes).

2 Drain and rinse the noodles in cold water; drain well, then toss with a little vegetable oil.

3 Heat the remaining oil in a preheated wok. Stir-fry the onion for about 30-40 seconds, then add the bean-sprouts and noodles, stir and toss for 1 more minute.

4 Add the spring onion (scallion) and soy sauce and blend well. Sprinkle with the sesame oil and serve.

FRESH NOODLES

Noodles are made from wheat or rice flour, water and egg. Handmade noodles are made by an elaborate process of kneading, pulling and twisting the dough, and it takes years to learn the art. Noodles are a symbol of longevity, and so are always served at birthday celebrations – it is regarded as bad luck to cut them.

If fresh egg noodles are available, these require very little cooking: simply place in boiling water for about 3 minutes, then drain and toss in oil. Noodles can be boiled and eaten plain, or stir-fried with meat and vegetables for a light meal or snack.

STEP 2

STEP 3

STEP 4

STEP 1

STEP 2

STEP 3

STEP 4

SINGAPORE-STYLE RICE NOODLES

Rice noodles or vermicelli are also known as rice sticks. Egg noodles can be used for this dish, but it will not taste the same. The ideal meat to use is Barbecue Pork (see page 16).

SERVES 4

200 g/7 oz rice vermicelli
125 g/4 oz cooked chicken or pork
60 g/2 oz peeled prawns (shrimp), defrosted
   if frozen
4 tbsp vegetable oil
1 medium onion, thinly shredded
125 g/4 oz fresh bean-sprouts
1 tsp salt
1 tbsp mild curry powder
2 tbsp light soy sauce
2 spring onions (scallions), thinly shredded
1-2 small fresh green or red chilli peppers,
   seeded and thinly shredded

1 Soak the rice vermicelli in boiling water for 8-10 minutes, then rinse in cold water and drain well.

2 Thinly slice the cooked meat. Dry the prawns (shrimp) on paper towels.

3 Heat the oil in a preheated wok. Add the onion and stir-fry until opaque. Add the bean-sprouts and stir-fry for 1 minute.

4 Add the noodles with the meat and prawns (shrimp), and continue stirring for another minute.

5 Blend in the salt, curry powder and soy sauce, followed by the spring onions (scallions) and chilli peppers. Stir-fry for one more minute, then serve immediately.

RICE NOODLES

Rice noodles are very delicate noodles made from rice flour. They become soft and pliable after being soaked for about 15 minutes. If you wish to store them after they have been soaked, toss them in a few drops of sesame oil then place them in a sealed container in the refrigerator.

VARIATION

For a really authentic flavour include 1 tablespoon dried shrimps, which have a strong, pungent taste. Soak in warm water for 30 minutes, drain and add to the noodles at step 4.

SPECIAL FRIED RICE

*Special Fried Rice, sometimes called Yangchow Fried Rice, is almost a
meal in itself. Make sure the cooked rice is completely dry and cold
before adding it to the wok, otherwise it might stick and become lumpy.*

STEP 1

SERVES 4

60 g/2 oz peeled prawns (shrimp)
60 g/2 oz cooked meat (chicken, pork or
    ham)
125 g/4 oz green peas
3 eggs
1 tsp salt
2 spring onions (scallions), finely chopped
4 tbsp vegetable oil
1 tbsp light soy sauce
1 tsp Chinese rice wine or dry sherry
    (optional)
500 g/1 lb/4 cups cooked rice

the rice and stir to separate the grains,
then add the remaining salt and spring
onions (scallions), and the prawns
(shrimp), meat and peas. Blend well and
serve hot or cold.

STEP 2

1 Dry the prawns (shrimp) on
kitchen paper. Cut the meat into
small dice about the same size as the
peas.

2 In a bowl, lightly beat the eggs
with a pinch of salt and a few
pieces of the spring onions (scallions).

3 Heat 2 tablespoons of the oil in a
preheated wok. Add the peas,
prawns (shrimp) and meat and stir-fry
for about 1 minute. Stir in the soy sauce
and wine, then remove and keep warm.

4 Heat the remaining oil and add the
eggs. Stir to lightly scramble. Add

FRESH PEAS

Fresh peas straight from the shell really do
make a difference to this dish. Their vivid,
emerald colour and just-off-the-vine
flavour make it worth the (relatively small)
amount of effort. Shell and lightly blanch
the peas before stir-frying them.

PERFECT RICE

Cook the rice by the absorbtion method as
described on page 78. Leave to stand,
covered, until the rice has absorbed all the
water, then turn out on to a large flat plate
or baking tray. Spread the rice out and
leave until completely cold and dry.

STEP 3

STEP 4

CHINESE COOKING

CHINESE STOCK

This basic stock is used in Chinese cooking not only as the basis for soup-making, but also whenever liquid is required instead of plain water.

MAKES 2.5L/4 PINTS/10 CUPS

750 g/1½ lb chicken pieces
750 g/1½ lb pork spare ribs
3.75 litres/6 pints/15 cups cold water
3-4 pieces ginger root, crushed
3-4 spring onions (scallions), each tied into a knot
3-4 tbsp Chinese rice wine or dry sherry

1. Trim off excess fat from the chicken and spare ribs; chop them into large pieces.

2. Place the chicken and pork in a large pan with water; add the ginger and spring onion (scallion) knots.

3. Bring to the boil, and skim off the scum. Reduce heat and simmer uncovered for at least 2-3 hours.

4. Strain the stock, discarding the chicken, pork, ginger and spring onions (scallions); add the wine and return to the boil, simmer for 2-3 minutes.

Refrigerate the stock when cool; it will keep up to 4-5 days. Alternatively, it can be frozen in small containers and be defrosted as required.

China is a vast country – about the same size as the United States – and its climate and food products are similarly varied. Consequently, each region has a distinctive style of cooking: no wonder China can claim to have the world's most diverse cuisine. Yet the fundamental character of Chinese cooking remains the same throughout the land: from Peking in the north to Canton in the south, and Shanghai in the east to Szechuan in the west, different ingredients are prepared, cooked and served in accordance with the same centuries-old principles. Some of the cooking methods may vary a little from one region to another, and the emphasis on seasonings may differ, but basically dishes from different regions are all unmistakably "Chinese".

The principles of Chinese cooking

What distinguishes Chinese cooking from all other food cultures is the emphasis on the harmonious blending of colour, aroma, flavour, and texture both in a single dish and in a course of dishes for a meal. Balance and contrast are the key words, based on the ancient Taoist philosophy of yin and yang. Consciously or unconsciously, Chinese cooks from the housewife to the professional chef all work to this yin-yang principle: harmonious balance and contrast in conspicuous juxtaposition of different colours, aromas, flavours and textures by varying the ingredients, cutting shapes, seasonings and cooking methods.

In order to achieve this, two most important factors should be observed: heat and timing – the degree of heat and duration of cooking, which means the right cooking method for the right food. This is why the size and shape of the cut ingredient must, first of all, be suitable for a particular method of cooking. For instance, ingredients for quick stir-frying should be cut into small, thin slices or shreds of uniform size, never large, thick chunks. This is not just for the sake of appearance, but also because ingredients of the same size and shape require about the same amount of time in cooking.

EQUIPMENT AND UTENSILS

There are only a few basic implements in the Chinese *batterie de cuisine* that are considered essential in order to achieve the best results. Equivalent equipment is always available in a Western kitchen, but Chinese cooking utensils are of an ancient design, usually made of inexpensive materials; they have been in continuous use for several thousand of years and do serve a special function. Their more sophisticated and much more expensive Western counterparts prove rather inadequate in contrast.

Chinese cleaver An all-purpose cook's knife that is used for slicing, shredding, peeling, crushing and chopping. Different sizes and weights are available.

Wok The round-bottomed iron wok

conducts and retains heat evenly, and because of its shape, the ingredients always return to the centre, where the heat is most intense, however vigorously you stir. The wok is also ideal for deep-frying – its conical shape requires far less oil than the flat-bottomed deep-fryer, and has more depth (which means more heat) and more cooking surface (which means more food can be cooked at one go). Besides being a frying-pan, a wok is also used for braising, steaming, boiling and poaching, etc. – in other words, the whole spectrum of Chinese cooking methods can be executed in a single utensil.

Ladle and spatula Some wok sets come with a pair of stirrers in the form of a ladle and spatula. Of the two, the flat ladle or scooper (as it is sometimes called) is more versatile. It is used by the Chinese cook for adding ingredients and seasonings to the wok as well as for stirring.

Strainers There are two basic types of strainers – one is made of copper or steel wire with long bamboo handles, the other of perforated iron or stainless steel. Several different sizes are available.

Steamers The traditional Chinese steamer is made of bamboo, and the modern version is made of aluminium. Of course, the wok can be used as a steamer with a rack or trivet and the dome-shaped wok lid.

Chopsticks Does Chinese food taste any better when eaten with chopsticks? This

is not merely an aesthetic question, but also a practical point, partly because all Chinese food is prepared in such a way that it is easily picked up by chopsticks.

Learning to use chopsticks is quite simple and easy – place one chopstick in the hollow between thumb and index finger and rest its lower end below the first joint of the third finger. This chopstick remains stationary. Hold the other chopstick between the tips of the index and middle finger, steady its upper half against the base of the index finger, and use the tip of the thumb to keep it in place. To pick up food, move the upper chopstick with index and middle fingers.

GLOSSARY OF INGREDIENTS USED IN CHINESE COOKING

Baby sweetcorn Baby corn cobs have a wonderfully sweet fragrance and flavour, and an irresistible texture. They are available both fresh and canned.

Bamboo shoots Available in cans only. Once opened, the contents may be kept in fresh water in a covered jar for up to a week in the refrigerator.

Bean-sprouts Fresh bean-sprouts, from mung or soya beans, are widely available from Oriental stores and supermarkets. They can be kept in the refrigerator for two to three days.

Black bean sauce Sold in jars or cans. Salted beans are crushed and mixed with flour and spices (such as ginger, garlic or chilli) to make a thickish paste. Once opened, keep in the refrigerator.

CORNFLOUR (CORNSTARCH) PASTE

Cornflour (cornstarch) paste is made by mixing 1 part cornflour (cornstarch) with about 1½ parts of cold water. Stir until smooth. The paste is used to thicken sauces.

PRAWNS (SHRIMP) WITH DIP SAUCE

300 g (10oz) raw prawns (shrimp), defrosted if frozen
1 tsp salt
1 litre/1¼ pints/4 cups water
2 spring onions (scallions), shredded
2-3 slices ginger root, shredded
2 green or red chillies, seeded and finely shredded
1 tbsp vegetable oil
2 tbsp light soy sauce
1 tbsp red rice vinegar
1 tsp sesame oil

1. Poach the prawns (shrimp) in boiling, salted water for 1 minute, then turn off the heat. Leave to stand for 1 minute, then remove with a slotted spoon and drain on paper towels.

2. Place the spring onions (scallions), ginger and chillies in a small heatproof bowl. Heat the oil until hot and pour into the bowl. Add the soy sauce, vinegar and sesame oil and stir well.

3. Shell the prawns (shrimp), leaving the tails, and arrange on a serving dish. Serve with the dip sauce.

PLAIN RICE

Use long-grain or patna rice, or
better still, try fragrant Thai
rice.

SERVES 4
250 g/8 oz long-grain rice
about 250 ml/8 fl oz/1 cup cold
*   water*
pinch of salt
¹/₂ tsp oil (optional)

1. Wash and rinse the rice just
once. Place the rice in a
saucepan and add enough
water so that there is no more
than 2 cm/¾ in of water above
the surface of the rice.

2. Bring to the boil, add salt
and oil (if using), and stir to
prevent the rice sticking to the
bottom of the pan.

3. Reduce the heat to very,
very low, cover and cook for
15-20 minutes.

4. Remove from the heat and
let stand, covered, for 10
minutes or so. Fluff up the rice
with a fork or spoon before
serving.

Chilli bean sauce Fermented bean paste
mixed with hot chilli and other
seasonings. Sold in jars, some sauces are
quite mild, but others are very hot. You
will have to try out the various brands to
see which one is to your taste.

Chilli sauce Very hot sauce made from
chillis, vinegar, sugar and salt. Usually
sold in bottles and should be used
sparingly in cooking or as a dip. Tabasco
sauce can be a substitute.

Chinese leaves Also known as Chinese
cabbage, there are two widely available
varieties in supermarkets and
greengrocers. The most commonly seen
one is a pale green colour and has a
tightly wrapped, elongated head – about
two-thirds of the cabbage is stem, which
has a crunchy texture. The other variety
has a shorter, fatter head with curlier,
pale yellow or green leaves, also with
white stems.

Coriander Fresh coriander leaves, also
known as Chinese parsley or cilantro, are
widely used in Chinese cooking as a
garnish.

Dried Chinese mushrooms (Shiitake)
Highly fragrant dried mushrooms which
add a special flavour to Chinese dishes.
There are many different varieties, but
Shitake are the best. They are not cheap,
but a small amount will go a long way,
and they will keep indefinitely in an
airtight jar. Soak them in warm water for
20-30 minutes (or in cold water for
several hours), squeeze dry and discard
the hard stalks before use.

Egg noodles There are many varieties of
noodles in China, ranging from flat,
broad ribbons to long narrow strands.
Both dried and fresh noodles are
available.

Five-spice powder A mixture of star
anise, fennel seeds, cloves, cinnamon
bark and Szechuan pepper. It is very
pungent, so should be used sparingly. It
will keep in an airtight container
indefinitely.

Ginger root Fresh ginger root, sold by
weight, should be peeled then sliced,
finely chopped or shredded before use. It
will keep for weeks in a dry, cool place.
Dried ginger powder is no substitute.

Hoi-sin sauce Also known as barbecue
sauce, this is made from soy beans,
sugar, flour, vinegar, salt, garlic, chilli
and sesame seed oil. Sold in cans or jars,
it will keep in the refrigerator for several
months.

Oyster sauce A thickish soy-based sauce
used as a flavouring in Cantonese
cooking. Sold in bottles, it will keep in the
refrigerator for months.

Plum sauce Plum sauce has a unique,
fruity flavour – a sweet and sour sauce
with a difference.

Rice vinegar There are two basic types of
rice vinegar. Red vinegar is made from
fermented rice and has a distinctive dark
colour and depth of flavour. White
vinegar is stronger in flavour as it is
distilled from rice wine.

Rice wine Chinese rice wine, made from glutinous rice, is also known as "Yellow wine" (*Huang jiu* or *chiew* in Chinese), because of its golden amber colour. The best variety is called Shao Hsing or Shaoxing from south-east China. A good dry or medium sherry can be an acceptable substitute.

Sesame oil Aromatic oil sold in bottles and widely used as a finishing touch, added to dishes just before serving. The refined yellow sesame oil sold in Middle-Eastern stores is not so aromatic, has less flavour and therefore is not a very satisfactory substitute.

Soy sauce Sold in bottles or cans, this popular Chinese sauce is used both for cooking and at the table. Light soy sauce has more flavour than the sweeter dark soy sauce, which gives the food a rich, reddish colour.

Straw mushrooms Grown on beds of rice straw, hence the name, straw mushrooms have a pleasant slippery texture, and a subtle taste. Canned straw mushrooms should be rinsed and drained after opening.

Szechuan peppercorns Also known as *farchiew*, these are wild reddish-brown peppercorns from Szechuan. More aromatic but less hot than either white or black peppercorns, they do give a quite unique flavour to the food.

Szechuan preserved vegetables The pickled mustard root is very hot and salty. Sold in cans. Once opened, it should be stored in a tightly sealed jar in the refrigerator. It will keep for many months.

Tofu (bean curd) This custard-like preparation of puréed and pressed soya beans is exceptionally high in protein. It is usually sold in cakes about 7.5 cm/3 in square and 2.5 cm/1 in thick in Oriental and health-food stores. Will keep for a few days if submerged in water in a container and placed in the refrigerator

Water chestnuts The roots of the plant *Heleocharis tuberosa*. Also known as horse's hooves in China on account of their appearance before the skin is peeled off. They are available fresh or in cans. Canned water chestnuts retain only part of the texture, and even less of the flavour, of fresh ones. Will keep for about a month in the refrigerator in a covered jar, if you change the water every two or three days.

Wood ears Also known as cloud ears, this is a dried black fungus. Sold in plastic bags in Oriental stores, it should be soaked in cold or warm water for 20 minutes, then rinsed in fresh water before use. It has a crunchy texture and a mild but subtle flavour.

Yellow bean sauce A thick paste made from salted, fermented yellow soya beans, crushed with flour and sugar. It is sold in cans or jars, and once the can is opened, the sauce should be transferred to a screw-top jar. It will then keep in the refrigerator for months.

CHINESE FRUIT SALAD

The Chinese do not usually have desserts to end a meal, except at banquets and special occasions. Sweet dishes are usually served in between main meals as snacks, but fruit is refreshing at the end of a big meal.

*250 g / 8 oz rock candy or crystal
    sugar*
*600 ml / 1 pint / 2½ cups boiling
    water*
1 large honeydew melon
*4-5 different fruits, such as
    pineapple, grapes, banana,
    mango, lychees or kiwi fruit*

1. Dissolve the rock candy in the boiling water, then leave to cool.

2. Slice 2.5 cm / 1 in off the top of the melon and scoop out the flesh, discarding the seeds. Cut the flesh into small chunks. Prepare the other fruits and cut into small chunks.

3. Fill the melon shell with the fruits and the syrup. Cover with clingfilm and chill for at least 2 hours. Serve on a bed of crushed ice.

INDEX